MOM:
MATRIX AND MOMENTS

Peculiar Medinus

Things evolve, and books evolve. There are autobiographies and biographies withering away on tired looking shelves, but this memoir will breathe an exciting wave of change and remain visible.

In loving memory of Molly Margaret Medinus Benibo

Copyright © 2023 Peculiar Pages Ltd. All rights reserved. Except for brief quotations embodied in critical reviews and certain other non-commercial uses permitted by UK Copyright law (Copyright, Designs and Patents Act 1988), no part of this book may be reproduced, distributed, or transmitted in any form or by any means, including photocopying, recording, or other mechanical or electronic methods, without the prior written permission of the publisher.

ISBN: 978-0-9956463-7-7

City Hill Press

www.cityhillpress.com

It's noontime in autumn, and while sitting at the corner of a coffee shop, I stare into a neatly served glass of white-hot chocolate. What is it about a cosy afternoon that makes the days go by faster? I have settled for an alternative remedy since the tin of Horlicks quietly sitting in my kitchen cupboard was ineffective. I've been caught up in bouts of insomnia. The autumn sun is shimmering through the window, failing to bathe me in warmth, and the only noise that fills my ears is the occasional tinkle of spoons against ceramic mugs. It feels as if time has stopped existing. There aren't many people around either, which makes for perfect solitude. I try reading a book, but my mind isn't in it. In fact, since my mother passed away a few days ago, reading has become quite a chore. Turning each page feels like another step away from her. Grief does that to a person, I guess. It creeps up on you when you're least expecting it and catches you off guard like an unseen thief in the night. In my view, every life has experienced grief. The first experience of grief was the first squeaky cry given while being born into a broken world. This was one of my grieving moments. Grief and pain embed us in emotions that we cannot explain. My mother's transition to a new life through death was not the reality of this grief; it was spurred by a sense of loss. Meaningful grief.

Everything seems grey, bleak, and pointless. Everything feels like a massive undertaking, except that I can ink my thoughts, and right here, in this coffee shop, I begin to write this memoir. Now, writing seems more appealing than ever; for me, it helps put things into perspective when life gets tough. I scribble away with determination in a cosy café, capturing an inner strength that contrasts with the feeling of gloominess.

Looking out of the window, I see the leaves falling gently to the ground like feathers. They swirl in the breeze before finally coming to rest. The warm yellow light of the café creates a soft and peaceful atmosphere, while the movement of the leaves brings an air of impermanence and change. It is then that I realise life goes on regardless of what happens to us. Molecules continue to move and interact long after we are gone. The world will keep turning, and perhaps I will overcome my grief with time. For now, I take solace in God through small moments like this, when everything else fades away and I am left with nothing but peace and quiet. Every so often, I find myself in moments of such serenity that words fail me.

Time slows, and the world stops spinning. I catch a mental picture of myself—looking out over a landscape that is both beautiful and sorrowful. My eyes rest on one of the falling leaves, depicting both the power and fragility of life and its transience while hinting at hope in spite of grief. I cannot escape into books as reading still sucks me into a world of misery. I am thankful that writing still feels cathartic.

I recently wrote a reassuring devotional on how to beat depression. But here I am, in its own confinement. Despite having the tools and knowledge of liberation close at hand, it seems as though the devil has hurled one at me. I have an inner warning to redirect a negative emotion and find my way back on track. However, on days like these, when the autumn sun shines bright and there's a nip in the air, I can't help but be reminded of my mother. Now, even though she's gone, her memory brings me warmth on cold days like these. There is beauty in pain and consolation even in sorrow. No matter how hard they hit me, I take it all as a blessing and am grateful for her life.

I see her in the way the sun shines through the trees. I hear her voice when the wind rustles through the leaves. In an autumnal atmosphere of nostalgia and comfort, my gaze *is* turned inward as I remember my mother with fondness. My memory catches a portrait of the mother with a smile on her face as if she were looking at me with approval.

I recall my mom's beauty—her grace and warmth radiating from every corner of her plump figure. Memories of her femininity remain deeply embedded in my heart. Her smile conveys a sense of warmth. My memory is flooded with images of significant moments framed in a warm golden hue, emphasising the love between us. I wonder what she would say if she were here with me now. She loved my writing and had always said to me, "I hope you're still writing." The words keep running through my head like a mantra. I think about what she would say if she were here with me now—something insightful, I think.

Right now, I feel energetic. I'm filled with hope and encouragement. When I feel most spacious, my mother's presence is palpable in a subtle way. I can sense her like a fragrant whisper, a comforting nudge that encourages me to take pause and reflect on the beauty of life. In moments of pain or sorrow, I am reminded that she, too, experienced moments of struggle but still managed to emanate an aura of profound love for those around her. She encouraged us to be grateful for her life and not let suffering and loss become ingrained habits in our souls. It grounds me in many ways, giving me permission to find peace amidst the sorrows of this world. I can still feel the embrace of her aura in moments of comfort or when I'm feeling overwhelmed by life's joys, frustrations, and sorrows. For these moments, I am reminded to be fully present, even if it's just for a few minutes each day, and to appreciate the beauty of life that she experienced and shared with me. Whenever negativity creeps in and tries to take over my thoughts, I take a moment to reconnect with this warmth and love, invigorating my soul with the hope that she, too, once embraced. This is where she truly lives—beyond this world and in my heart—encouraging me to be strong when life seems overwhelming. The memories we shared always remain close, like the photograph album casually tucked away on the corner shelf. When I glance at it, there's an immense reassurance that our relationship was real and true. It was so vivid with colour that its beauty almost aches my heart. Through conversations and laughter between us two, our bond still radiates with each passing day, nourishing my spirit ever since its inception.

I know Mom's spirit lives on every page. She was such an inspiration to me. I was devastated at my mother's passing, even though it was not untimely as some would say. She had been such a central figure in my life. Writing this memoir would be a way to keep her memory alive and remind me of some wonderful moments we shared. Even though she is gone, her love remains. The process of writing has been therapeutic for me. And through my words, I hope to give others a glimpse into the wonderful person she was.

The autumn sun, which failed to offer me warmth, has suddenly gone down. I grab my cup and take the first sip of my chocolate drink. The deliciously sweet flavour seems not to provide an escape from this roller coaster of emotions, but I have more than an illusion of contentment. I was hoping that some time spent alone outside might be a distraction, but I don't have a lot of it. Even though it feels comforting, there is also an underlying sense of loss mixed with hope. As my gaze moves around the cafe, it seems as if everything holds an emotional significance. As I watch the people around me carry on with their lives, I can't help but feel detached. I decide it is time to leave the coffee shop. Reluctantly gathering my belongings, I leave with memories dancing through my head. I hear snippets of conversations echoing through my mind as I slowly walk away.

Matrix

Mom laughed heartily after I told her that Dad had called me "typical Molly!" while we were on a short holiday. My younger mind could only grasp "normal" or "ordinary" as the meaning of "typical." With a perplexed expression, I looked at my mother as she chuckled heartily with a knowing twinkle in her eyes. My mother's reaction locked me into a deluge of thoughts. It felt like a tonne of giant marbles were juggling inside my head. Was there something deeper that, as a child, I couldn't comprehend—some sort of special meaning behind Dad's words? I wanted answers. Why was Mom laughing instead of hissing with disapproval? Was there a deeper meaning that a child could not decipher? With the inquisitiveness that accompanies an early teen age, I needed to grasp Dad's real reason for calling me "typical Molly." But the unexpected reaction from Mom lodged me into further curiosity. It was curiosity that earned me the knowledge of the matrix as a casting mould.

The cast is typical of the bearer of the matrix. I missed out on approaching my strict dad to get the gist of "typical Molly," but I opted to delve into reflections that disclosed "typical" as one of many examples. However, after giving it some more thought, I realised "typical" can also mean "characteristic" or "distinctive." In other words, my dad could mean I'm "typical Molly" because of my hearty chuckles. Similarly, my mom might say that my sister is "typical Georgina" because she's always as organised and tidy as my grandmother. I got a clearer picture. Dad was calling me "typical" because he had seen something familiar to Mom in me —something cast through the same matrix! It's funny how dads always seem to be able to characterise their children with just a few well-chosen words. How do they always seem to capture the essence of who their children are in such an effortless way? What would it be like to eavesdrop on a heart-warming conversation between fathers about their children? These dads know how to make each other's hearts swell with joy and laughter, from proud, boastful stories of accomplishments to shared moments of humorous misadventure. Ah, what wonderful conversations they must have!

My dad was particularly proud when it came to his children. His eyes lit up every time he spoke of us. His gentle, fond tone brought back the vivid memory of an amused expression on his face as he called me "typical Molly," and that's fine by me. I'm proud to be "typical Molly"!

As it turns out, his words were meant in admiration. I'm inclined to agree! Proudly wearing my badge of honour, I'm content knowing that when people think of Molly, they reflect on her positive contributions and personality traits that are noteworthy, all things summed up by the label "typical Molly."

Had I exhibited a behaviour that was so quintessentially me that it paid homage to the entire Molly brand? My curiosity to uncover the meaning of the "Molly brand" was ignited by a single answer. I humbly learned the meaning of one of the different breeds formed in my mother's matrix. Mother gave birth to nine children instead of ten, having miscarried one of the twin babies. I concluded that Dad referred to a kind of Molly in a collection of typical Mollys.

Despite the shy smile that later settled on my mom's face, I would have mustered up the courage to ask why she found Dad's comment so amusing. Mom would have looked at me with tender eyes and told her story or asked me to get the answer from the horse's mouth—which meant speaking directly with Dad himself.

Well, why regret failing to get straight answers? Curiosity had already given me the light bulb that lit up in my head, and the phrase "typical Molly" took on a whole new meaning for me!

My tongue stuck between my teeth as I examined this moment and concluded that Mom gave a resounding cheer at the realisation that Dad missed her.

With this new insight, I could make more sense of Dad's reference than ever before. As these thoughts coalesced, I also sensed with absolute certainty that Mom would have embraced Dad's missed attempt at humor. I can now see the lighter side of Dad's joke, which had previously escaped me.

Sitting in my sunlit room with my head tilted to the side while I mulled through my thoughts, I had a mixture of sadness with a hint of fondness. The moment was tense and uncomfortable, but the sound of Mom's voice broke through it like a ray of sunshine. My eyes widened with realisation as I tried to process what this meant—would things be different now? There had been such a long separation between them. Love really can make anything possible!

With a newfound understanding came an overwhelming wave of emotion that filled my heart with warmth and love for both of my parents. I felt something unexplainably incredible when I began to comprehend the depth of my parents' relationship. They hadn't been together since I was seven. Even after all those years apart, there remained a powerful connection between them that filled me with warmth and adoration. It made me feel connected to them. Mom and Dad shared an indescribable bond built upon mutual respect over many years—it was truly special! It was a separation without divorce.

Here I am, walking through a turbulent storm with determination while unseen rays of warmth wrap around me like an embrace from within.

I have my own sense of style without having to conform to societal expectations or norms; there was something exhilarating about being able to do what felt right without worrying about what others may think or say. What's more is that I found solace in taking risks and pushing boundaries—it made life far more interesting!

Have you ever chosen to go against the grain? While not following the crowd brought some unique perks, it also presented its fair share of challenges, like dealing with criticism and learning how to best handle difficult situations when they arise. Yet, despite these struggles, I embraced them as part of who I am—they were just other obstacles on this wild ride we call life!

In the end, being "typical Molly" was something special, a reminder that each individual is unique in their own way and should be celebrated for embracing their quirky selves regardless of outside judgement or opinion. And if Dad saw fit to honour this part of my personality by calling me "typical Molly," well then, it just goes to show I can still be proud, even when I don't quite fit the mould!

But then another thought occurred to me—something swirled around in my head. I noticed something strange happening inside me—something that felt oddly familiar yet distinctly new at the same time. It almost felt as if a part of me was coming alive! Nothing else could explain why everything within me suddenly felt so awakened, so energized, so alive! Then suddenly, it hit me: I'm living proof of how powerful individuality truly can be.

What clarity! It almost seemed like an old, familiar friend who had re-emerged from the depths to reignite my spirit. It dawned on me: This is what happens when you unleash your unique power. My experience has truly shown how powerful our individual identities can be if we just let them shine through with boldness and conviction.

Every person you come across offers something valuable. Take the time to appreciate and learn from each individual, no matter who they are! We often assume that those around us are just faces in the crowd, but there's something deeply special under their surfaces. Even if it goes unnoticed, we all have qualities and characteristics—an intriguing combination. It pays to take a closer look. We'll find a collection of skill sets, talents, and past experiences that make us one-of-a-kind.

With this newfound understanding in hand, I realised that we are all special in our own way. Even if we seem typical at first glance, there's always something about us that makes us stand apart from others. In other words, we all get cast through our unique matrix.

My mother's matrix was a developmental context, and the safe environment God chose for my protection. It was the first point of our meeting and the place she held the secret of an upcoming breed before it became public. In cognition, it was the special place divinely arranged by the source, the foundation, and the genesis of growth. It was God's designated space for His uniquely carved destinies. It was the womb for embryonic development during birth, being endowed with the capacity to host embryos from conception. As an intrinsic part of human existence, it was the divinely planted seedbed for growth, the micro-space for creation and miracles, and the purposeful space for creation's mission. It was a gift from heaven, divinely prepared to shape destinies. It was the sacred space for germination and gestation during life's creation.

It's incredible to have a place of comforting refuge. I was in awe of this special place, uniquely arranged just for me, appointed by God to be the haven for *me* moments before being unveiled and presented on this world's stage. It served as the launching pad for me to come to fruition—a beautiful cocoon I call home. Inside, there was such power and potential, providing the ideal environment for life-affirming growth and development. God's grace resides within each person He created. What a truly miraculous blessing!

It must have been quite something for one not just to witness its origin but also to even imagine what prospects and realities it could bring forth.

Have you ever experienced the power of a mother's love? For me, it was like being embraced by an unwavering current as I navigated through life-changing moments. My mom's matrix served as my safety net, with all the joys accompanied by pain.

Mom's matrix, rather than slavery, was a channel of protection outside of which I cried during the birthing process. "Protection from what?" you might ask. From the world. From pain. From hurt. From disappointment. From all of the things that can go wrong in life. Everything—physical harm, emotional distress, and relationship troubles—were all met with understanding and shelter in her infinite capacity for comfort. In spite of life's complexities, I had a guardian who could preserve both my physical and mental safety during these moments when I needed it most. God blessed me with a sheltering channel of comfort that could protect me. This guardian provided solace no matter how turbulent things had become, shielding my well-being in times when it felt as if nothing else could save me from an uncertain future.

As a figure curled up in the foetal position with my eyes closed tightly, I was encircled by God's angels, protecting me from the chaotic elements of life depicted around me with stormy clouds and crashing waves. God also protected the vessel, my mother, from unseen dangers on her pregnancy journey.

I felt a deep, emotional connection to my mother's womb even as I ventured out into the world and discovered new things. It was in this matrix that I was formed. Leaving her loving embrace was heart-wrenching yet inevitable. Our souls were still linked despite years apart, and only we could understand these depths of emotion, which couldn't be expressed with mere words.

Moments

*A*fter the birthing process of my mother's matrix, we had moments. Moments that did not quickly disappear but exuded the mind of the matrix. Outside the matrix, the human replica formed from an embryo goes through the developmental stages, being nurtured from milk to solid food. Being hatched into existence in an independent life form, I was in my "swimming" period, and as an infant, I received Mom's continuous protection and had the necessary supplies to help me survive until adulthood. My "swimming" period as an infant was crucial for my survival.

As I began to explore this brave new world around me, my mother watched over me with a protective love that made me feel safe no matter what happened. Through each stage of growth, she provided for me until adulthood loomed on the horizon like a beacon of hope and possibility. Those months when everything seemed strange yet familiar at the same time; when every experience was novel yet comforting; when I could practise survival skills outside the womb before bringing them with me into adulthood. My swimming period gave way to moments full of wonderment and curiosity as I tried to make sense of this unknown part of life that lay ahead for me now that my time within

Mom's cocoon was complete. And while some days brought fear or sadness, there were also days filled with joyous memories from my past that blended seamlessly with present experiences—memories that served to remind me why being nurtured by my mother's unconditional love had been worth it all along.

For the first few weeks of my life, I drifted with the current, relying on breastmilk. Mom was providing me with plenty of love, attention, and nutritious food. Through my mother's breastmilk and the enzymes it contained, I was protected from diseases and infections with plenty of love, attention, and nutritious food. It was easy for me to digest. Breastmilk proved to be a powerful ally for me as an infant. It promoted healthy gut flora in addition to fighting infection and disease with its antibodies. As such, I was shielded from developing allergies and chronic illnesses. I was immensely blessed that this incredible source of nutrition was available at such an early stage in my life—something so natural yet powerful enough to give me these kinds of benefits. I am thankful to God that Mom provided this extremely valuable resource just for me out of her immense love and affection towards her baby girl. My parents had nothing but love for me. They gave me so much attention and care. It was such a special time in my life.

All I knew were the feelings of warmth, comfort, and security.

As I grew older, I began to explore my surroundings and soon discovered that there were other creatures like me—some larger, some smaller. I learned to adjust to my new surroundings while getting used to the bright lights and loud noises of the world around me. I was also exposed to different people, places, and things aside from learning to feed, sleep, and poop on my own. However, it became more natural to me over time, and eventually second nature.

I became exposed to everything, from what kind of food we ate or which language we spoke at home to how our days unfolded each morning until nightfall when it came time for bed again. Everything felt strange yet familiar all at once; it was weird but comforting too.

The nature of a moment cannot be defined by an equation that compares hours, minutes, and seconds in numerical terms, nor can its significance be determined by the mere expression of the number of breaths taken per unit of time and the fractions of a second allotted to each inhale. Amid our busy days, we forget to appreciate that each moment is a precious gift.

Sometimes, life moves slower, and moments seem to last forever. Everyone should use the luxury of time to appreciate each moment, savouring each breath and counting every second as if it were the most precious gift that could be received. No matter how hard we try, we can't put a numerical value on something as special as a moment. Let's take some time out today to appreciate every single moment before it slips away forever!

It follows that reality, rather than numbers or dimensions, provides the best definition of a moment. I can feel the wind blowing through my hair and against my skin. It's a cool breeze, but it doesn't quite reach down to my soul. The world spins around me. For a moment, everything is perfect. Then reality crashes down on me like an unwelcome guest at a party.

I closed my eyes and took a deep breath. I opened my eyes to find myself alone, with nothing but thoughts whirling through my head to keep me company. My perfect moment has been replaced by something that feels far more mundane, despite the beauty all around me. What does it mean for something to be beautiful? Is it simply what we can see with our eyes or feel with our skin? Or is there something more complex beneath the surface—some intangible quality that makes it special? Beauty is much more than what meets the eye; its depths lie within, in kindness and compassion. True beauty radiates from deep within one's soul. How do you quantify "perfection" when perfection itself isn't easily defined? The wind swirls around me again, prompting another deep breath from within before slowly fading away again into nothingness, leaving only peace behind in its wake as if it had never been there at all.

I would get lost in calculations, trying to make sense of the world around me. But now I realise that reality is what's important. It surrounds and defines us, whether we acknowledge it or not. And sometimes, when you're fortunate, you catch a glimpse of it. I'm just living in the present, experiencing reality as it is.

Reality is life's simple beauty without all the added layers and complexities—if only for a few moments, at least—if we choose to live in the present instead of dwelling too much on our pasts or worrying about our futures; if we take time out each day to appreciate life's little miracles that are happening around us every single moment; if we open our eyes a bit wider and observe these simple realities without letting them pass us by unnoticed.

So now I'm living differently than before, savouring each experience as it comes and making sure no single moment passes by unappreciated. Reality is here with us every step of the way, defining who we are regardless. But sometimes, catching those precious glimpses gives us an even deeper understanding of who we're really meant to be and what kind of lives we're truly meant to lead.

I opened my eyes, and the first thing I felt was a deep sense of loss. I can't help but feel that something is missing. I wake up expecting to hear my mom's sweet voice, but she's not there. I reach for the phone to give her a call but realise that I can't. We used to talk frequently on the phone, but now the silence is deafening. I took a deep breath, and it seemed to echo in the room as if it were travelling through time itself. It had been a few weeks since she passed away. Only God's strength can fill this gaping hole in my heart.

Reality provides the best definition of a moment, and it's far more complex than anything I could ever measure or calculate. Every moment seemed to be filled with a deep complexity that defied explanation—as if reality itself had an unspoken language only visible through careful observation. I thought back to my days growing up, when life was simpler but felt so much more meaningful. There were moments that seemed to last forever no matter how hard time tried to pass by: moments where sparks flew between people, when laughter echoed off walls, or when tears fell down cheeks without warning or reason. It just was what it was, raw and beautiful in its own way. But now the world around me felt different somehow—almost as though those precious moments had been washed away by the tides, with loved ones fading away over time. It's simply up to us to appreciate every single second that passes by as if it'll never come again, because who knows what tomorrow will bring?

It's funny how we spend our lives chasing after things: money, fame, and power. We think they'll make us happy, but they never do. It's not about achieving them and having them in abundance; it's about realising that you already have something greater than anything money can buy. For me, that something is God.

Life has taken me on many paths and steered me down roads both good and bad, but through it all, right here, right now, my one true anchor is God. When everything else around me seemed uncertain or chaotic, His presence was always there to give me strength and hope for the future. It may sound strange, but I'm thankful for the struggles I went through because now I understand how truly blessed I am with faith in God as my constant companion throughout this journey we call life. He is always by my side, no matter where I go or what happens—nothing can break our bond of loyalty and love! Even when times are tough, He gives us reminders that He will never leave us alone. He always shows us how deeply we are loved unconditionally, whether it is through an unexpected blessing from Him or a kind gesture from someone else. We spend far too much time worrying about material possessions, instead of focusing on cultivating relationships with the people who care about us most: family members, friends, and most importantly, God Himself. In doing so, we miss out on living our lives to their fullest potential—being content with ourselves and enjoying each moment without worry or stress over things beyond our control. At least, that's why knowing Him has made such a difference for me personally in finding happiness within myself at last, no matter what comes next in this wild adventure called life.

The older I get, the more I realise that time is precious. It's something that we can never get back, and it seems to be slipping away faster and faster as each day goes by. There are moments in our lives that are far more significant than the amount of time that passes between them. Those moments are what matter most, and they're worth more than anything else in the world.

It was a normal day in my life—nothing out of the ordinary. I woke up and went about my morning routine. But something felt different today; there was an underlying sense of urgency that seemed to be tugging at me from all sides. I couldn't quite put my finger on it, but it made me feel uneasy. Every passing minute brought with it a wave of anxiety that seemed to linger just beneath the surface. I found myself thinking more and more about how time is fleeting—how quickly years pass by without us ever truly appreciating them while they're here. It's easy to get caught up in our daily routines without taking a moment to appreciate what we have right now before it slips away forever into memory or oblivion. Each moment is precious; each second has its own unique beauty, no matter how mundane or insignificant it may seem on the surface. If you take some time to look closely enough, you can find beauty even in those moments that are too often overlooked or forgotten completely once they've passed us by. No one knows when their last breath will come. With that knowledge comes a newfound appreciation for living life fully, cherishing every single second we have left on this earth before we turn into memories ourselves. So, let's make sure our memories are worth remembering!

I always think about the moments with my mom. I was looking forward to visiting again when I join her to watch her favourite TV shows: The Talk, Dr. Phil, Judge Judy, and Young and Restless. Sometimes, I feel like an incomplete puzzle missing its most important piece. I miss hearing her laugh and seeing her smile. I miss talking to her about everything and nothing. But I know that she's in a better place now and that I'll see her again someday. Until then, I'll cherish the memories we had together. It's hard to believe that she's gone, but I know she would want me to keep living and be happy. So that's what I'm going to try to do. Even though it's hard, I know that she would want me to keep going. All I can do is keep living and making memories of my own while cherishing hers forever in my heart.

It's hard to believe she's gone, but despite the sadness I feel deep down inside, there are moments when a spark of happiness returns as fond memories come back to me: times spent just sitting quietly side-by-side, enjoying each other's company without needing any words at all. In those moments, tears don't fall from my eyes, but she is always alive within my heart.

Time marches on relentlessly, but special moments stay with us forever. The significance of a moment far exceeds that of a length of time because it holds an infinite amount of value that cannot be put into quantitative terms. Yet, time is endless and unfathomable. Despite how fast time seems to be moving, some moments stay with you forever. No matter how much time passed or how far those memories were in the past, they still felt as fresh and vivid as ever.

There's something infinitely special about spending time with a loved one. A loved one who passed away in autumn, when the leaves were starting to change colour and the trees were beautiful against the bright blue sky. The crunch of leaves and the wind blowing through the branches reminded me of Mom's visit in autumn a few years ago. She had repeatedly mentioned the forceful wind blowing through the trees when we talked on the phone.

I always find myself drawn to this time of year. It had something infinitely special about it. This particular autumn was especially memorable for me; no matter what we discussed, she would often stop mid-sentence, pause, and then say, "What's that sound? The breeze is strong out there!" There was an invisible bridge connecting two hearts separated across two continents yet brought closer together than ever.

I paused for a moment, taking it all in. I felt so fortunate to have my mom visit despite her ailments. That moment is something that I'll never forget, and it's valuable to me. The silence between us remained unbroken for what seemed like hours but passed only seconds later when Mom finally broke it by speaking softly: "How are you doing?" She looked up at me with eyes full of wisdom and smiled reassuringly before continuing, "God is not asleep. He will meet you at every point of need." This struck me deeply, and I remind myself just how valuable this moment truly is. She was always encouraging me and believed in my creative abilities.

Old memories resurfaced from moments spent with my mother when I was young: conversations, hugs, goodbyes, even when I got a spanking... All of these bittersweet memories came flooding back, one after another.

"I remember the day you were born vividly," Mom told me. "A bright light flooded your grandmother's world, and she had a joyful fall while coming to meet you."

My grandmother gave me unconditional love and walked me to school as an infant. It was the early stage of her glaucoma, but she still made me delicious meals and rocked me to sleep.

To fully grasp the significance of a moment, one must first recognise and comprehend the various contexts in which it can arise. I recall the day my grandmother died like it was yesterday. Mom had to explain what happened, and I remember having a good cry. It felt like time stood still, but life went on. I quietly watched my mom handle grief with strength. She allowed me to accompany her to the mortuary to see her mother's lifeless body. It's been so many years now, but I still remember the love and care of my grandmother. Sometimes, I laugh at the memory of dancing gestures, folktales, and singing. Grandma had glaucoma, but love shone through her blindness. Frequently, she would ask me to bring her small wooden box, opening it up eagerly with anticipation of something new within its depths every single time. Though blind, Grandma would look at me with kindness in her eyes, as if she could see through my soul. She would hand me a piece of fabric printed with beautiful designs that carried entire tales behind them. "Take it to the tailor to make you a new dress," she'd say. It was only after she had passed that I realised the enormity of what she had done. I miss her more than words can express. I never thought those moments with Grandma would be some of my fondest memories. I guess the takeaway from all of this is that we should never take our loved ones for granted because you never know when they might be taken away from us. Life is precious and fragile, so we should cherish every moment we have with those we care about. Even though time has passed since then, I still feel grateful for every moment we shared. What a great lady Grandma was, whose legacy will live on forever in my heart despite not being physically present anymore! Thanks to Grandma's kindness reverberating within my heart with every step forward.

Unique encounters create moments. I had always thought that experience was the ultimate teacher. And, in a way, it was. Experiences are a compilation of emotions, feelings, sensory perceptions, and knowledge gained in ways unique to every individual. Although we have a definitive understanding of what constitutes an experience, it is impossible to create an objective definition for every experience because every individual has different circumstances, emotions, and feelings that engage different senses and provide varied knowledge.

Every encounter taught me something different, each one creating its own moment in time that could never be replicated. These moments created powerful memories. Was my appreciation for unique experiences born out of an innate curiosity or something else entirely? No matter how hard I tried, some questions seemed destined to remain unanswered. But maybe that was okay too. After all, not all journeys are meant for finding answers but rather for discovering new paths you never thought existed.

Sometimes, I take things at face value and move on, not dwelling on the past. But now, as I sat alone in my room, I couldn't help but reflect on certain moments—the ones where something unique happened—something that could've taught me a thing or two about life. The silence was so loud that I could hear every thought that floated through my mind. I'm deciding not to take things at face value anymore but rather search deeper into any situation or person, looking past the surface level towards something much bigger than what meets the eye. And if anything ever did seem too good to be true, then instead of pushing away those feelings of doubt or confusion right away, I would take some time out first before making any decisions, just like someone said: "Don't rush into anything until you're ready or understand enough about it!"

I remember the little things about my mom: how she could make a simple meal taste as if it came from a five-star restaurant; how her hugs seemed to have healing powers; how her laugh lit up any room she entered. But more than anything else, what made my mom so special was the way in which she loved us unconditionally and selflessly. Every moment spent with her felt like a warm breeze on a cold winter day—comforting yet fleeting at the same time, as if it wanted to remind you just long enough of all those beautiful moments when your mother surrounded you with love and protection right when life tested your courage most harshly. No matter what happened in our lives, no matter where we went or who we encountered along the way, my mom was an anchor for us. She never wavered from her commitment to guide us through life's storms while ensuring that we would always emerge stronger and wiser than before despite them. Her strength seemed to transcend physical boundaries because nothing ever truly managed to limit this constant source of comfort that only a mother can provide, even though everything around us appeared subject to change due to its very nature being limited by dimensions such as time or space. There are no words that can adequately describe just how much I miss my mom's presence now, but one thing is certain: anything with dimensions has its limits. It could be measured, weighed, compared, and quantified, but Mom was an exception. Mom's unmatched qualities mean she will forever remain priceless in our hearts! I don't mean it as a compliment; it is true.

Have you tried to keep track of moments of uncertainty?

At times like these, when everything seems so uncertain and out of control, it's worth reflecting on moments of joy and trying desperately to cling to them. This really matters in life and makes it worth living amidst all the chaos. No matter how hard things got though, no matter how much darkness with which I was surrounded, one thing remained constant: hope. I try to focus on the good moments, even when darkness seems to be creeping in. It's good to hold on to hope. It's good to hold on to tiny glimmers of light.

I remember the morning I got the call. My mother

had passed away. The pain, the confusion, the disbelief. It was like a tight fist around my heart, but there was light. Learning to transcend pain, I seek connection with something greater.

It felt surreal, as if my world had been turned upside down, and all of a sudden everything felt unfamiliar. My mother had passed away, and for a moment, it didn't register. There was nothing but pain—an intense feeling that spread through every inch of my being like wildfire, burning me from within. Confusion quickly followed—what happened? Why did this happen? How could I cope with such devastating news?

But in spite of the overwhelming grief and fear, there was something else too: light shone through the darkness that threatened to consume me whole. Although life would never be quite the same again without Mom's presence, I found solace in knowing that she touched so many lives during her time on Earth—mine included. Even after she physically left us, her spirit remained ever present in our hearts and minds.

The loss of my mother made me appreciate life more deeply than ever before, to take joy from each passing day no matter how small or insignificant it may seem at first glance, and to embrace love unconditionally even when it hurts because we can never know what tomorrow will bring. These are the lessons I learned long after that fateful phone call changed my life forever.

Life is made up of moments—big and small, fleeting or everlasting. Some moments are remembered forever; others are quickly forgotten, but all the same, they pass us by like grains of sand in an hourglass. I truly understood what it meant to be alive—to experience life in its fullest form with no regrets or worries about the future because everything we need is already here within us if only we take some time out of our busy lives to pause and appreciate each moment as it passes us by. It's funny how these moments can seem insignificant at first but, upon reflection, can become such powerful memories that define who we are today.

My mother's lasting legacy is more than just memories; it is a warm embrace of love that carries me through life. In her absence, I draw strength from the time we shared together and take comfort in knowing she shaped my character with so much tenderness and grace. From her beautiful smile to teaching me right from wrong, Mom showed me how to live life fully by example rather than words alone, blessing those around us with inner strength, love, and empathy every day. Her loving spirit still shines brightly on Earth, while Heaven looks down upon us in awe at all the lives she has touched along the way.

MOM

We may not realise it now, but every minute detail matters. Most moments shape our experiences and give meaning to our lives.

We should never forget how precious life really is! Life is made up of moments.

Here are the moments...

Motherhood

Motherhood is a journey that looks different for everyone. For some, it's a beautiful and natural experience full of wonder and love. For others, it's a more difficult road, marked by challenges and sacrifices. But no matter what, motherhood is always worthwhile.

Pregnancy follows months of dedication—learning new things each day about parenting while struggling against exhaustion like never before. It isn't always easy or straightforward; every now and then there are moments filled with frustration or even sadness over something that didn't turn out quite right along the way.

Some say being a mom is the most important job in the world, and without a doubt, motherhood is a miracle. After nine months of being cooped up, it feels good when friends, family, and acquaintances offer their congratulations.

Being a mom is hard work, but it's also incredibly rewarding. There's nothing quite like watching your children grow and learn; seeing them experience their firsts is truly wonderful. From first steps to first words, from learning how to read to making friends at school.

The labour may be long and hard, but it is joyful

when the baby arrives safe and sound. The mother looks down at her child with love and wonder and knows that she would do anything for this little one. Thankfully, my mother was always with me and provided me with everything I needed until I grew into an adult.

My mother was a strong and resilient woman. She had been through many hard times, but she never let them bring her down. My baby brother passed away a few days after birth. I remember her working nonstop for days on end until the baby arrived safely and soundly. Dad took me to the maternity ward, and the joy that filled the room was overwhelming as my mother looked lovingly at her new bundle of joy. The feeling of pride and accomplishment radiating off of her was palpable. She had done it—she had brought another life into this world with nothing more than sheer willpower, determination, and faith in God.

She was a teacher, a counsellor, and a friend. She was strong when I was weak, loving when I needed it most, and always there for me no matter what. She showed me what it meant to be a mother, not just through her words but through her actions. I hope that by sharing my mother's story, other women will be inspired to follow in her footsteps and become the best mothers they can be. My goal is to show that it is possible to be an amazing mother. It's also about being an amazing role model, even without being married or having kids yourself.

I am eternally grateful for everything Mom has taught me throughout our lifetime together. Her invaluable guidance is something to strive towards, so future generations will greatly benefit from such positive examples set by inspiring mothers like mine.

My mother was an exemplary caretaker who followed the biblical command to "train up a child in the way he should go." My mother is gone now, but she has left a legacy of faith in the hearts and minds of her children. Her selfless guidance and unwavering support have propelled her children to become role models in many areas of life. Nurturing and the effect she has on the hearts of her children are illustrated in what I remember most: her prayers and her everyday loving example. In her daily prayers, my mother never neglected to pray for her children and their families—sons, daughters, grandchildren—everyone who needed special attention from Heaven. From my earliest childhood until her last days, she would close her eyes and ask God to bless each one of us. In her hands, all of us were recipients of great care and concern. She would often say to me: "Stay close to your siblings, and may all of you be content and live long lives, being happy,

Motherhood

healthy, and prosperous." And her final words to me at the end of each telephone call were, "May the Lord preserve you, protect you, and help you." On the eve of her death, my mother was still thinking of her children, and God remained the centre of her life. Motherhood is a gift from God, and my mother was a living example of that. She was strong in her faith, and her love for her children was unending. Even in death, she continues to be an inspiration to me and my siblings. Her prayers continue to be answered in our lives today. Motherhood is a vocation that should be treasured, and my mother was one of those mothers who truly understood what it meant to be a mother. "A mother's love is like a rose; its beauty radiates from within." My mother was a beautiful person, inside and out. She radiated the love of Christ, and I am grateful to have had her as my mother. As I look back on my life, it is clear that her commitment to raising me in the way God intended has had a lasting impact, even after she's gone. Her prayers have transcended time, as they echo through eternity into the present moment and fill my heart with hope and peace.

I will forever be grateful that, through faith in Jesus Christ, love conquers death, so we are never separated from those we cherish beyond this world. What an incredible gift it is to know that mothers are truly angels here on Earth whose influence lives long after their physical body passes away.

I know that I have to keep going for her sake. She would want me to be strong and live my life to the fullest. But it's so hard when every little thing reminds me of her. It all feels like a dream. But I know that she's in a better place now and that I will see her again one day. Until then, I will keep her close to my heart and cherish the memories we have together.

My mom was a great cook. When I was young, I would help her in the kitchen, and we would make delicious meals together, stirring pots, chopping ingredients, and tasting the flavour of each dish as it simmered away on the stovetop—a combination of vegetables and spices, all cooked together with love. The smell of those delicious stews lingered in the house long after they were gone. While cooking this recipe, I smell that same aroma now, and I am taken back to those times with my mom, and the grief comes flooding back.

Almighty God, the loving owner of children, has given mothers a sacred responsibility to guide them securely amid the tumultuous seas of human life. Raising a child is a beautiful opportunity to bring honour and glory to the Creator.

Even the woman whose life has turned out in ways she had not anticipated should embrace motherhood.

Motherhood

Motherhood is biological. It is also a calling. Motherhood is a beautiful experience that can bring unparalleled joy and fulfilment. It's an opportunity to nurture another being—a calling too special for words!

Satan's goal is to demolish the vital roles of motherhood, both on a biological and spiritual level. But no matter how hard he may try, there are women who are resilient forces in this world that will always persevere!

Being a mother is so much more than just maternity; it's an incredible and rewarding journey that extends beyond the physical experience. There are many different aspects to being a mom: nurturing your children with love, teaching them how to be their best selves, and showing them what life has to offer. The possibilities really are endless! We are not just responsible for our own well-being; we also owe it to God and others around us, including children in need of love and protection. By obeying Him, we can show that respect and provide the care so many deserve.

Motherhood begins at the moment of conception, which is not mainly physical. It goes beyond having children, which is what it most empathetically is. When rightly undertaken, it moulds us into the compassionate people we are. Women who are unable to experience motherhood in a physical way have an opportunity to fulfil this role. They can be just as successful and influential as those who have undergone a pregnancy journey.

How wonderful it is that women who don't have a biological bond with their children can still be the best, most loving mothers at heart! Women play a divinely important role as both spiritual and biological mothers, making them an indispensable part of God's grand plan.

Women don't have to be mothers biologically to reach out, show love and guidance, and help shape the future of those in need. Let's harness our compassion for others as a way to make real change!

Mothers are a powerful and unsung source of strength that shapes us into the adults we become. Their invaluable lessons about perseverance and courage in the face of difficulty make them indispensable family members. Through their motherly guidance, women can find purpose in life and belong to God's divine plan; they are truly an incomparable blessing! I am particularly thankful for my mother's unwavering wisdom.

Motherhood is a special journey that offers profound spiritual rewards for women. With each milestone in their children's growth, mothers can experience an enriching transformation of their faith and character. With the love of mothers and guidance from above, children are truly blessed with an amazing combination that leads to success.

A Christian woman epitomises motherhood, showering her children with unconditional love, faith, and courage. She carries a torch of hope that illuminates any darkness that stands in the way of her family's progress. Through her gentle guidance, she has an immeasurable impact on those around her, teaching them to look up for strength as God blesses them with courageous hearts! Her legacy is one of righteous womanhood that future generations can rely on. There will always be someone willing to stand firm just like their beloved mother did before them, radiating heaven-sent love through timeless affection whose effects are felt throughout life's journey, providing comfort no matter how far away they may wander from home.

A mother's guidance is a blessing to behold—one that I have experienced and been incredibly fortunate for. My amazing mom was the epitome of God's grace, having shaped my life in all the best ways imaginable. With an overwhelming sense of sadness mixed with immense gratitude, I testify that her teachings stay strong within me today.

Dress Sense

My mother would often make me go to church. I was a little girl, no older than eight. Every Sunday morning, we would rise early and head off to the local house of worship. I remember feeling so out of place in that grand old building—it seemed never-ending, and the air was thick with respect and reverence. I would sit in the pews and listen to the preacher drone on about sin and redemption. Distracted, I would look up at the stained-glass windows. The sunbeams shone through them with such vibrancy. Sometimes, I'd make friends at the children's Sunday school who shared my sense of wonder for this strange new world. These friends often convinced me to sneak off to the sweet shop nearby afterwards!

Even though many years have passed since then, those memories still bring warmth into my heart whenever they come back into focus: a little girl wrapped in faith yet captivated by something far greater than what meets the eye—freedom through friendship and laughter amidst infinite possibility... and sweets!

I remember that day as if it were yesterday. I had been so excited to get ready for church, but I also knew that it could be a daunting task. My mom always took the initiative to help me out and make sure everything was perfect. I needed help getting ready for church.

She ditched her hand into a bunch of jewellery and pulled out two round earrings to clasp my tiny wrist, which could not hold her oversized bangles.

"These will do," she said, looking at my dainty little hands.

With an affectionate smile, she added, "Get ready in good time. We don't want to be late."

Pulling out the trunk box, she brought out a thick traditional cloth and skilfully tore it into two, as the whole bundle would be too heavy on my waist. She tied the cloth around my waist and knotted the two edges so it would not drop off.

Mother had a variety of white, pink, and multi-coloured stone laces, which her skilled tailor had trimmed to my size. She took out the beautifully trimmed lace tops and asked me to pick a colour that matched the traditional cloth on my waist.

I thought for a while before deciding on a beautiful white lace top.

After making my choice, Mother helped me carefully into my lace top, ensuring that the lace had dropped down properly to cover the knob on my waist.

When she was finished, she tied a smaller piece of

cloth over the lace and helped me put on the rest of my native church attire. I was really touched by her actions and felt really blessed to have her as my mother. After we finished putting on my church attire, she looked at me and said, "Your clothes sit well on you." She folded the headgear in a simplified way to tie around my head, and I wore two small dangling pieces of gold earrings that flapped my chubby cheeks. She looked at me and smiled with such warmth and said, "Be careful not to lose those gold earrings."

Opening her purse, she gave me a bunch of coins to put in the little handbag that matched my shoes. "Those are for church offerings," she said softly. It was harvest time. I was the lead singer in the children's harvest choir.

As I approached the church building, I could feel my heart racing in my chest. I tried to take deep breaths to calm myself, but it was no use. I knew what was coming. And there was nothing I could do to stop it.

The air was thick as people gathered in the church to celebrate this special day and give thanks to God for His many blessings. I was also very excited because I would be leading our children's choir during service, singing praises to God amidst all His abundance!

I didn't know then that my mother's faith would be such an important part of my life. Years later, when I was struggling to make sense of some difficult circumstances, I turned to her example for strength and guidance. It all started when I faced a particularly challenging period in my own life. I felt lost, alone, and overwhelmed by uncertainty. Every day seemed like an uphill battle as I tried desperately to make sense of everything going on around me—until one day, out of nowhere, this incredible feeling came over me. It was almost as if someone had taken me by the hand and said, "It's okay." And suddenly—just like that—the fog lifted away from my mind and heart, leaving behind a newfound clarity about what really mattered most in life: kindness towards others, lasting relationships, hope for brighter days ahead, but most importantly, faithful trust in God, no matter what comes our way.

Now, as an adult, I am so grateful for the foundation she laid in my life. Every time I put money in the offering plate, I think of her and the lessons she taught me about faith, charity, and gratitude.

Mom would sit quietly in the corner of the church and watch me lead the children's harvest choir with my chest pressed against the pew. Mom was a woman with a reserved demeanour who would let her blessings announce themselves without opening her mouth. She would simply bend her head and give a smile that showed a beautiful parting on her cheeks when complimented on my performance. Mother, while grateful for the gift of her child, was unimpressed. Her intention was not to be proud of the gift. She had a physical dress sense embedded in a goal to introduce me to a spiritual dress sense. Mom had a mission to shape my spirit and give me the tools I needed to stay strong in my faith.

Mother would give anything for my involvement in church activities. She dressed me up for church better than she did for any other occasion. It was always a special occasion when my mother dressed me up for church. I'd slip into the silky fabric of each carefully chosen outfit with an air of anticipation, the way one feels on Christmas morning or at one's birthday party. Even though I was only eight years old, I could sense that these outfits were more than just clothes; they were symbols of my mother's faith and her hope that one day soon, I too would be a believer in God.

I remember one particular outfit. It was a pink dress with frills around the waist and pretty lace detailing around the neckline, making me look cute. She believed that if I looked good, I'd feel good and be more likely to participate in church activities.

Mom was a woman who did not confuse church with God but had a relationship beyond the spheres of religion. She taught me how to look up. I grew up thinking there was more to life than religion. God is not confined to a building or a set of beliefs. God is love, and love is everywhere. We can find God in the simplest things: a smile from a stranger, a kind word when we're feeling down, and the beauty of nature.

True faith goes beyond blind acceptance or judgement; instead, it's about having an open heart and mind for all the experiences life has to offer.

> *Mother, I watched those quiet moments when you sneaked out of bed during the most terrifying hours of the morning.*
>
> *Just as the hen spreads out her wings over her chicks at night after a tireless search for them by day, you gave with your hands by day and with your heart at night.*
>
> *It's been many years now and your knees are never tired!*
>
> *You chose the posture of submission, but your heart reached Heaven as you whispered to God to protect your children.*
>
> *You did not only kneel for your own; you also kneeled for others.*
>
> *You are the prayer warrior who wrestled to crush satanic strongholds.*

> *You are the woman who pleaded for lives to be spared from evil.*
>
> *On your knees, you still stand in the gap for others.*
>
> *As I lay in bed pretending to be fast asleep, I peeped with an open eye and vowed: "I must take her cue!"*

Readers of my book, *The Female Preacher*, already know those words sit on the dedication page. There's no iota of exaggeration. Mother dressed up spiritually before the dawn of each day. She dedicatedly knelt by her bedside and said her prayers before daybreak. It was a spiritual dress sense from which I took a cue. My mother started each day by getting dressed with prayer. The room's doors and windows never opened until she had dressed up spiritually with prayers.

From the way my mother dressed each day with prayer, I also began to understand the need for spiritual discipline in my life. Just as it is important to physically dress up each day and take care of our bodies, it is also important to dress up spiritually and take care of our souls. By "dressing up" spiritually, I mean taking time for personal prayer, Bible study, and reflection on God's Word.

Dress Sense

My mother was an amazing woman. She had a quiet strength that I could never understand, yet every day she would rise out of bed at the darkest hours of the night to kneel before God in prayer. It seemed as if no matter how tired her body felt, her heart still found the energy to reach up towards heaven and ask for protection for our family and those around us. I watched in awe as my mother prayed for countless people whose lives were on the brink of destruction due to satanic strongholds or other evils in their lives. Even though she'd been through so much herself, she still had enough love left over to plead with God on behalf of others—and it worked! People's lives changed because of her prayers and faithfulness; they were saved from what could have been their ruin. Kneeling is a posture of submission, but when we do it faithfully before God, His answers are sure, even if we don't see them right away. To this day, I'm inspired by my mother's example and strive to follow after her covenantal faithfulness, kneeling down whenever I need guidance or help from above!

Amid the chaos of life, it is essential that we take a step back and create space to listen carefully for God's still, small voice. When we neglect our spiritual lives, we become susceptible to all sorts of temptations and spiritual attacks. But when we are spiritually strong, we are better able to resist temptation and stand firm in our faith.

So, if you want to start your day off right, follow my mother's example and dress up spiritually with prayer. You will be amazed at how much difference it makes in your day and your life. Entrust your future to the power of prayer and sow its good seed everywhere. Mother's prayers worked in my life and in the lives of others. Those prayers have not only silenced the enemy but have also given us victory. I have seen opened doors that seemed impossible to open and broken chains that seemed impossible to break. God holds the key to every door, but He won't unlock them unless we open our hearts and invite Him in, and the quickest way to do so is to meditate on His Word. The Bible offers a steady source of guidance and hope. Its timeless wisdom carries us through any storm we may face in life.

I could always count on my mom, who'd sit for hours reading passages and soaking in each word as if it were precious gold. I used to love watching her, quietly taking in all she was doing without disturbing her routine. My favourite memory of her will forever remain etched into my heart: reading the Bible before breakfast every morning with such devotion and sincerity that it brought tears to my eyes just looking at how much faith she had placed into each scripture she read. Faith was the guiding light for Mom—a conviction that God's will drove all of life's obstacles, and His Word led her through them.

Without an inner focus on spiritual growth, it can be hard to find the joy, contentment, and belonging that make life meaningful. Striving towards such goals could help unlock a deeper level of fulfilment than we knew was possible.

Harbinger of Peace

Mom was priceless, with a reserved demeanour and an inner strength that inspired me. Her death depicts her gentle and quiet nature. God truly gives His beloved sleep (Psalm 127:2). She passed away in her sleep to God's heavenly bounty.

Sometimes I would just break down crying, but I know she is in a better place now, and that gives me some comfort. I believe God called Mom home to heaven because He needed another angel by His side. She was such a gentle and quiet person, and she always radiated peace. I know that she is now watching over me from heaven, and I am grateful for the time we had together on earth. I will cherish our memories forever.

I will never forget the priceless gift of having such an incredible woman as my mother—one who showed true inner strength throughout everything she faced in life—until eventually being called home by God Himself.

My mother had a mysterious aura that captivated everyone who encountered her. Her spirituality helped her give an abundance of love and positivity. She was a model of fortitude and had the courage to stay firm

Harbinger of Peace

when faced with trials. Instead of fighting, she armed herself with peace and serenity, knowing that God would take care of everything. Though her silence may have been perceived as weak, she was, in fact showing courage by refusing to be drawn into a conflict. Mom was a master of her emotions, never letting even the most trying circumstances provoke an emotional reaction. She trusted in the Lord's unending strength during times of trouble and was confident that He could see her through anything without any additional aid from her.

No matter what people attempt to do, their actions cannot alter God's predetermined outcome. His power and mercy are beyond comprehension—a redeeming force that nothing can overpower or stifle. I have learned this valuable lesson: when we choose to ignore God's plan and go our own route, it can have severe consequences. God's plan is perfect, and even in the face of adversity, He will not leave us. For those who love Him and strive to live for His purpose, God can bring good out of any situation! It is wise to stay within the boundaries of divine instruction. When we put our faith in the Lord, we know that no matter how dire a situation may seem, with Him by our side, all is not lost. It is always better to surrender to His will. By connecting with the divine source, we can enrich our connections with others and bring greater harmony to all of our relationships. Mom did it!

Contentment

Even though times were tough, my mother's wisdom and guidance instilled in me the virtue of contentment. In dire circumstances, she held us to a high standard, encouraging ambition while tempering it with humility. I revered my mother for modelling the virtue of human dignity. She was consistent when I faltered. I wanted my mother to buy me a doll from a shop as a young girl who has outgrown infancy. I was so desperate to get the doll that sometimes I walked up to the storefront and gave it a stare. But mom didn't get me the doll despite my tantrums. She made me realise I needed chalk and slate instead of a doll. And then, on a quiet evening, my worried mom helped me exhale a piece of chalk, which I shoved up my nose while she helped me write numbers on a chalkboard. Mom taught me how to differentiate between want and need, which helped shape my understanding of material value as I grew into adulthood. She was humble, yet not small-minded. I was not subjected to rejection or pressure, as some parents do with their marriageable daughters. Rather, she gave me a word of caution and fervently prayed for

God's best course for my life. Above all else, her utmost concern was that I would make wise choices, both in who I surrounded myself with and in what values I chose to uphold throughout life's journey. Contentment is something that now resonates deeply within my heart whenever I am faced with difficult decisions or challenging times. Whenever I'm feeling overwhelmed or uncertain about what lies ahead in life's journey, her wise teachings come back to remind me just how powerful contentment can be—not only financially but mentally and spiritually too.

I can see that those with the glitziest of exteriors are not necessarily as content and fulfilled inside. With God's help, I'm learning not to let material possessions dictate how much value or worth I feel, recognising that comparing oneself in such a way would only lead to an unquenchable thirst for more—never enough satisfaction gained from all the things acquired.

My mother was content with what God gave and resorted to good budgeting through the period of austerity when she did not earn a salary for almost a year as a matron. She raised crops through outsourcing on a staff-allocated plot to accrue passive income. She was diligent and dedicated and lived within her means. It was a difficult time for my mother. She wasn't making much money as a matron at the school. But she never complained, no matter how tough things got. She was always content with what God gave her, even when things were tough. She made sure that we had enough food to eat and clothes to wear. And she would pray every day for God's guidance in our lives.

She never lost faith, no matter what the circumstances were. And I admired her for that. She never acted entitled or let her circumstances get her down. Mom remained positive and upbeat. It hasn't always been easy, but eventually, I learned to appreciate the value of contentment. When I was younger, I didn't understand how she could maintain such a cheerful attitude, but as I grew older, it began to make sense to me. Even with very little money or resources, Mom taught me that contentment is key.

Sometimes, we forget to appreciate the good in life. Instead, we become fixated on what we lack. Taking a moment to count our blessings can help us realize just how much is still going right! It's human nature to want what we don't have, but following one of the ten commandments (Exodus 20:17) reminds us that life is not about comparing ourselves and our possessions with others. Instead, it encourages us to be content with who we are and with the resources God has given each

Contentment

of us. To reach true contentment, it is essential to embrace the spiritual side within ourselves. Without taking this step, we find that our lives are filled with an unending sense of unease.

My Mother, My Friend

Mother taught me the essential tools I needed to build a fulfilling life. In an era of mass manipulation, knowledge serves as our ultimate defence against those that try to shape us into whatever they want. By remaining informed and aware, we can stand tall in the face of any attempt at control and know exactly who we really are.

My mother believed that knowledge and understanding would have a significant impact as I navigated life's challenges later on. She turned to alternative methods of teaching me as I became stuck in a seemingly endless naivety. She also wanted me to read more, be able to think more critically about life, and appreciate different perspectives on relationships rather than blindly going after whatever society dictates. She introduced me to the book that made her cry.

Beyond Pardon, written by Bertha M. Clay (a pseudonym for Charlotte M. Brame), is an old novel with a writing style that differs from modern romance novels that will be considered improper to read. I scanned through it quickly. It seemed like exactly what I'd enjoy reading. The contents relayed the message of love and treachery with no foul language. *Beyond Pardon* is a fictional story about infidelity and its impact on interpersonal relationships. My mother, having carefully observed the sanguine character traits I displayed at a young age, introduced me to fiction that would be less boring to read. I found myself engrossed in the story, rooting for the character who struggled to overcome mistakes. My mother wanted me to understand that one of the unpleasant realities of life is that your loved ones will disappoint you. God has the power to lead us to the point when we must deal with the repercussions of deliberate or unintentional sin. Those were the two things my mother wanted me to learn. Although it was difficult to read about the heartbreak and betrayal that the characters experienced, I appreciated my mother's effort to introduce me to this engaging novel. It was an eye-opening experience that helped me understand the complexity of relationships and human emotions. Against the odds, my mother showed me how to truly see and recognise my worth. In protecting me, Mom tried to make me realize that what may seem good at the moment could be detrimental to our long-term well-being. She gave me the strength to believe that God had something bigger and better in store for me than what desperation or impulses might suggest. Through faith and trust, she affirmed that if we strive to approach life while embracing God's values, the result will be bountiful blessings from Him. Her unwavering guidance has been integral to leading a life of discerning wisdom as I reach towards fulfilment.

What would it be like to pay your mother a surprise visit? A few years ago, my older sibling and I kept my visit a secret from Mom. My heart was racing with anticipation of her reaction as I walked up to her as she sat at the dining table. Suddenly, there was an expression of shock mixed with delight on her face. She quickly recovered from her surprise and embraced me. It was a few months before Christmas, following the death of my brother, Prince. We spent an amazing time together talking about all that had happened since we last saw each other: the happy moments, the sad moments, and everything in between. It felt so good to be able to share everything with someone who understood exactly what I went through without judgement or criticism.

On what ended up being my mother's final days on

earth, I spent time talking with her about our shared memories and reminiscing about happier times from our past together as a family. We both laughed at some wonderful memories, which brought with them the warmth of nostalgia while also reminding us of just how precious life is.

Love and Care

Mom was my champion, and I will never forget the selfless love she showed me each time I needed her most. My memory danced through remarkable moments with Mom. Even when illness threatened, mom fiercely protected me; I still have a mental picture of mom shivering while she carried me on her aching back to rush me for treatment. On a quiet day while we were at home, I suddenly became sick and fainted. She demonstrated her unwavering dedication to protecting me. It began to drizzle not long after we left our house, but Mom didn't hesitate or slow down; instead, she kept going despite the pouring rain, which almost drenched us. Her determination was inspiring, even in such dire circumstances! It serves now as a reminder of how much strength lies within us if only we can muster up enough courage to face our challenges head-on, no matter what they may be—something I'll never forget!

Mom was the parent I lived longer with. On a lonely day, she helped escort me on my first steps away from home with tenderness. She accompanied me across the river on the boat from our island town, having bought me enough food to take me through the journey. My mother was a caring woman who raised children who were not blood relatives and was very accommodating when it came to babysitting her grandchildren. My mother's unconditional love for her children was a gift that kept on giving. That devotion resulted in countless special moments between us and later extended itself into offering parental guidance as the matron of several institutions.

Despite working hard every day and having to raise their own children, my parents took in other children over the course of their marriage, many of whom were dealing with difficult situations. Mother's heart was also big enough to welcome countless others into our home. She embraced them all with love and compassion, helping me develop a strong empathy for others—something I'm eternally thankful for. Growing up with a mother blessed by an unbeatable maternal instinct, she made sure her own daughters never fell prey to unjust abuse or manipulation. But that wasn't enough for her; in addition, this amazing matron devoted herself to being the protector of other people's daughters as well.

Whenever times were tough and I needed guidance

or desperate solace, she always had a way of knowing precisely what to do. Sometimes she would make me dinner when I was feeling down, and many times she gave me much out of little. Her actions spoke louder than any words ever could. They were capable of communicating more deeply just how much she cares about me, even from afar.

I never really understood why my mother was so reticent with her words until I became an adult. Now I realize that it's because words are often inadequate to express the depth of our emotions. Sometimes the most important thing we can do is simply be there for someone, offering our silent support and love. Take some time today to remind your mom how much you appreciate the incredible gift of selflessness she has bestowed upon you.

Who could imagine a mother's valiant efforts to make her daughter's wish for long hair come true? Mom was forced to make a long plait out of my short hair to meet my demands. Through sheer determination and ingenuity, she was able to craft this solution that made me happy! How incredible is it that even when we were young, something so simple yet meaningful conveyed so much love from one person?

Every holiday season, my mom would buy me a new

dress. It was something that I looked forward to each year, and the secrecy of it made it even more exciting. She'd go shopping and pick something special for me, then get it out for me as a surprise. I value those moments. They are some of my most cherished memories with her.

COURAGE

Courage and fear exist together; one cannot thrive without the other. In order to be brave, we must also feel a degree of trepidation. It is in this tension that true courage emerges.

Some years ago, Mom sprang into action. Quickly and quietly, she tiptoed to pick up a long stick, raised it very high, and gave a heavy hit to an object, which turned out to be her belt. My heart pounded in terror at the mysterious shape. I had woken my mother from a quiet sleep at midnight because I saw a long, curly image in the dark and panicked, thinking it was a snake. My heart raced as I watched, and she quickly assessed the situation and realized that it wasn't some dangerous creature after all. Upon realizing no snakes were lurking about, my heart rate gradually returned to normal, and it became evident just how bravely she'd handled the situation.

It was an encounter that we both laughed about after a few years, but I give her tribute for her courage. It was an unforgettable incident of a mother protecting her child. I look back with admiration and awe at how bravely my mom reacted in such an intense situation. In many ways, my mother was a selfless and caring hero. Her beauty, courage, and intelligence are immeasurable. My mother's willingness to take a risk to safeguard me will remain one of my enduring memories.

Mom's return home after long rehabilitation was a miracle in itself. With her incredible determination and courage, she slowly but surely left the wheelchair and was back on her feet with the aid of a Zimmer frame—an inspiring sight that left all those around breathless. The health practitioners were amazed to see Mom back on her feet, giving her an infectious smile. I admired her for her bravery and dedication. From days to weeks, my mother worked hard at physiotherapy until finally achieving what felt impossible: climbing stairs.

Everyone faces tedium at some point in life, but we must never forget that having faith helps us make it through. Even when the situation feels overwhelming and hopeless, courage will provide us with the strength to activate our trust in a better tomorrow. Mom would never bother anyone about personal matters, but the moment came when she needed assistance. A moment of personal care for a parent counts as a privilege. I paused with a deep appreciation for my older sibling, who had most of those moments. Taking off my hairband to hold my mom's soft hair, I remained her little girl. Mom still treated me as her little girl. Not long afterwards, she made a shush as I talked. Just the way a guardian would tell an infant, "Keep quiet!" I had laughed at the memory of my mother telling me, "I'm old now." And then she'd tilt her head towards me, so we took a selfie.

Testimony

My mother had encounters that would have sentenced her to an early grave, but a satanic ploy to ditch her family into tragedy proved abortive. The devil employs strategies to weaken the faith of Christians, but God always intervenes. I've had conversations with my mom in which she recounted how God saved her life many years before I was born. My mother was the friend who would chat with me and give me moral lessons from past and present encounters. Every time the enemy tried to derail her from faith and family, God stepped in and saved her. It was not storytelling; she wanted me to boost my Christian faith and assure me that God is dependable as I journey into the future. My parents have learned the great value of the Christian faith through their positive experiences. They understood that the Christian faith is more than just a set of moral values; it is a positive relationship with God and trust in His guidance in all aspects of life. The most valuable lesson I learned from my parents was to follow the path of Christianity. Their continual testimony about the Christian life was a rich source of insight for me. My mother was not a megaphone preacher; her peaceful, quiet, and gentle spirit preached God to others. Her exemplary life served as an impetus for me to live out my faith in front of others. She was a role model and my key teacher of the Christian life.

As she stood in the countryside, disappointed by a delayed journey, my mother did not have the hindsight of great deliverance from the snare of death. In her desperation, she did not discern God's preservation. She found herself in a situation where she persisted in getting something but never got it, and it turned out to be a miraculous rescue for her. She wanted to make her journey in a commuter's vehicle but had less than the full fare. The driver had bluntly refused to negotiate a lower fare.

My mother did make her journey. She could afford the next vehicle's fare. A few miles away from where her vehicle took off, she saw that there had been an accident involving a tanker and the commuter vehicle she couldn't join. The same vehicle that refused to take her had collided with a petrol tanker, and everyone on board was killed. The lifeless victims lying before the gawking eyes of spectators were the same passengers who had stared as my mother bargained. My mother was awestruck by God's deliverance, despite her anguish over the loss of those people. God preserved my mother's life and constantly shielded her from the treacherous schemes of the adversary. I reflected on the incident and was reminded that God honoured His Word in Psalm 91: "He who dwells in the secret place of the Highest shall abide under the shadow of the Almighty... He shall cover you with his feathers, and under his wings you shall take refuge; his faithfulness shall be your shield and rampart. He shall give his angels charge over you, to keep you in peace; and they shall bear you in their hands, lest you dash your foot against a stone."

My mother was always a very strong woman. She faced some pretty tough challenges in her life, but she never gave up. Even when things looked their darkest, she had faith that God would see her through.

As a young girl, I always looked up to my mother. She was strong, kind-hearted, and always put others before herself. But what I admired most about her was her faith in God. My mother never preached to me, but she lived out her faith in front of me every day. Her quiet strength and gentle spirit spoke volumes to me.

This incident taught my mother to be grateful to God for His protection. It also made her realize that there are some things that we think we want but may not actually be good for us. Sometimes, what we think is a delay or setback may turn out to be a great blessing in disguise. When we find ourselves in challenging situations, it is important to remember that God is always in control. We may not be able to see His hand at work in the midst of our trials, but we can trust that He is working everything out for our good (Romans 8:28).

Even though we may not understand why things are happening the way they are, we can be confident that God is sovereign and He knows what is best for us. So the next time you find yourself in a difficult situation, remember that God is in control. Trust that He knows what He is doing, and He will work everything out for your good.

GRIEF

Experiencing loss can have a major impact on one's mental health, leading to feelings of deep sadness similar to those reflected in depression. Both grief and depression create emotional distress that should not be taken lightly. Depression can be an isolating experience. Due to a lack of understanding, those who suffer from it often feel trapped in their own minds. Misconceptions around depression have created a barrier between society and this debilitating condition, leaving many struggling in silence without support. Depression can be a devastating and insidious illness that slowly erodes one's faith in oneself, wreaking havoc on one's physical, mental, and emotional well-being. It can have profound effects on people's ability to lead a fulfilling life by fracturing relationships, instilling self-doubt, and causing immense pain. While physical ailments may cause pain and suffering, mental health issues such as depression can be even more difficult to endure due to the invisible nature of this battle. God is our source of strength in difficult moments, offering the courage to persevere despite any obstacles. My mother made me

Grief

understand that God is a better friend to someone who is grieving. With God as an ever-present ally, no obstacle is too daunting to prevent a person from achieving recovery. I have seen Mom at different grieving times. When life threw her curveballs that felt too heavy to bear alone, she turned to God in prayer. I can still remember those moments—the sound of her soft voice as it echoed through our house and the warmth of her comforting embrace afterwards. It brought me solace knowing my mom could turn any tragedy into an opportunity for faith, no matter how devastating the situation may have been. She placed her heart in the hands of God, who can touch where no one else can. God's hands can settle things that are not fixable on earth. They provide peace where chaos reigns and hope where despair has taken root.

The first adult cry I witnessed was my mom's. I was only three, and she held me in her arms while she wept as my grandmother consoled her. She had just been told that her firstborn son, Emmanuel, had passed away suddenly and tragically. At that moment, it felt like the entire world had come crashing down around us. We were surrounded by an overwhelming sense of grief and sorrow as I tried to make sense of what had happened. The death of her first son, Emmanuel, left a void, but my mother's strength became evident in a way I'd never seen before or since then. Despite everything she'd gone through—the pain of losing not only her own son but also other children and grandchildren; the death of her mother; even the passing away of my father some years later—she always chose to stay strong and resilient, instead of succumbing to despair or being consumed by self-pity or bitterness. She learned to take heart, recognising God's unforeseen purpose in times of pain and suffering. She chose to trust God with an open heart to His will, never lost hope in the face of difficulty, and was in no way self-righteous or pious.

My parents taught me how to take heart no matter what happens in life; how to recognise God's unseen purpose amidst suffering; how to trust Him when things seem darkest; and, most importantly, how to not be discouraged from pressing forward regardless of failing or succeeding along your journey because, either way, He will bring good out of it eventually.

The world has its own mysterious way of presenting us with hardships and taking away the ones we need at our most desperate moments. My mom showed great courage during hard times, crying at moments but remaining hopeful, which is something I admired about her.

Grief

Grief is a process, not an event. Though painful at first glance, those feelings can actually lead us towards healing if we take our time with them instead of pushing them away too quickly before allowing ourselves space for proper growth and understanding along the way. There are different types of grief. The type that comes with the death of a loved one is the most difficult kind of grief. However, the type that comes with temporary changes is hard to deal with but is not permanent. Tears are a natural part of the grieving process, and it is okay to cry. Everyone grieves in their own way and at their own pace. There is no timeline for grieving. Some people may seem to be over their grief quickly, while others may take much longer. Grief can be very difficult to deal with, and it is okay to reach out for support through counselling or support groups. Even though the pain of grief can be overwhelming, there is always hope for a better tomorrow. When we lose someone we love, they are never really gone. They live on in our memories and hearts. Pain can be an unwelcome companion, often driving away those we need the most to offer care and comfort. My mother made me understand that God is a source of strength in the midst of our pain. Grief makes us appreciate the good moments in life and be more compassionate towards others.

I never saw Mom shed a tear in anger or frustration, only in pain and sorrow. In the face of death and loss, she always held on to hope. She inspired me to be strong in the midst of difficulties and to trust God, even when things are tough. My mother taught me the value of faith, hope, and strength. Through her example, I have learned that it is okay to cry when things are tough but that it is also important to remain hopeful and trust God through everything.

How have you navigated the rollercoaster of emotions that comes with grief? One minute, I feel fine, and the next minute, I am hit with a wave of sadness. In the haze of days that follow this sense of loss, Mother's voice still echoes in my ears from the last night we spoke. I had rejected the news of my mother's death and reiterated with a message, "Sisi is not a corpse." I talked with my mom at 23:27 hrs on the 2nd of October, and the news that she had passed away a few hours later locked me into shock and denial.

It didn't take long before I started emulating this sense of strength and hope within myself. After all these years since then, I still find comfort in knowing that amidst any difficulty or challenge we may face together in life—be it joyous or painful—we can still rely on one another's support just as much as we can trust God's comforting grace through everything else. Feeling a

Grief

divine presence melts away sorrow. God uses His kind gaze to mend. Joy awaits those who seek God's presence. Turning away from sorrow provides a gateway to experiencing His greatness. Psalm 16:11 offers insight into the promise of divine joy that can be accessed by all.

Two October Sundays

On an October Sunday, my mother gave birth to me, her new baby girl. Within weeks, our eyes met for the first time as she cradled me in her arms. Our gazes locked, and we just stared at each other. It was like we both knew that this was it—this was the beginning of a special bond that would last a lifetime. At that moment, I felt like I knew my mother, even though I had never met her before. No words needed to be spoken; no questions needed to be asked.

And then the years rolled by. On a Sunday night in October, I had the urge to call my mom. The phone line was engaged each time I tried calling, which only made me more determined than ever to connect with her. It was late at night, but I could not resist the urge to keep calling. After many attempts and much persistence, I had a breakthrough. My mother's unique voice came through. We talked, and I was sated. I'm glad I gave in to the urge, because it was then that I had my final moment with the channel God used to give me life.

Our earthly meeting and parting were divinely orchestrated. At 11:27 p.m. on the 2nd of October, we talked, and at 9:31 a.m. on the 3rd of October, news came that she was gone. My mother was the first person I met on an October Sunday and the last person I spoke to on an October Sunday.

Death

I woke up to an email from my sister saying that Mom had a lesion in the aorta and was rushed to the hospital. My heart sank, and I felt helpless as I wasn't able to be there for her physically. Thoughts of fear, worry, and doubt raced through my mind until I remembered to trust God for what would happen next. An aortic dissection was required for the lesion to be removed, and Mom was in intensive care. I prayed and trusted God for a supernatural surgery, as I thought my mom was not strong enough for a physical one. I was relieved at the news that doctors decided on an alternative way to remove the lesion instead of performing physical surgery. It was a great delight to know Mom had been moved out of ICU. While out of ICU, I spoke to Mom on a Sunday night, but got the news the next day that she had passed away peacefully in her sleep. I've always believed God has His own plans, even though things don't always turn out as expected. He works wonders every day if we open our eyes wide enough to see them unfolding around us.

With her body racked by pain, she was fully aware of the imminence of death and unfazed by it. She passed away peacefully, and she is now free of pain and sickness. The Christian faith is a joyful and fulfilling one. My mother had a protracted illness, but the faith she embraced so wholeheartedly gave her the inner strength to accept the inevitability of suffering and allowed her to face death with dignity. While our hearts were weighed down, Mother's courage never faltered, even when faced with such finality. We were comforted by knowing how secure she felt in the Christian faith, which held so much promise for those who believed wholeheartedly as she did. In life, there may be an upper limit on determination, but my mom's Christian faith remained unshakable. To the very end, she remained a woman of prayer. There is perseverance, but human perseverance has limits. In denial, I dialled phone numbers to connect to my mom. I refused to accept the death.

Death is a rebirth into life in a spiritual world, but it is definitely not an easy thing to deal with. It's the loss of the body while the spirit lives on. Though losing my mother's physical presence is hard, I know she still lives on in spirit. And through memories, which are more than just thoughts, I can feel her love more than ever.

Mom has left behind some amazing memories that will always stay with me. She was graced with so many inner strengths and qualities that made her an amazing person. She touched the lives of many people with her compassion and friendliness, and I believe she's watching over me from heaven now. I'm so grateful for all the wonderful moments we shared together. They're truly life-changing realities that I'll never forget.

Sometimes, you can't keep the people who mean the most to your life from coming and going. I know this sounds bleak, but it's true. There will always be a piece of my mother with me, whether in her words or actions (or both). Though she is gone now—nevermore shall we see each other again—I am grateful for all that she taught me because, with God, my soul is guided through these dry and heavy days.

My birthday had a different character as the day witnessed the sighting of a casket with my mother's body. I missed my mother's birthday blessing and cancelled my planned holiday in her honour. It was her service of songs. Due to distance and short notice, I was not physically present in Massachusetts, but the service aired live. I was able to watch virtually with people whose presence still felt tangible. Some people won't be there all the time but will be there at remarkable moments. My heart was heavy, and the tears flowed out uncontrollably. Carol held me tight, not minding my tears dripping on her, pulling out more tissues to replace the drained ones. And then there was a rotation of warm hugs. It was Blessing and then Margaret, giving their warm hugs and muttering comforting words and prayers. Sorrow hung in the air, and everyone else present took in the mood of the moment.

I'm grateful to friends and relatives who helped turn my lounge into a flower shop and a card factory. They sent messages expressing love through bloomy reminders, and some were there to give me hugs and prayers to comb away my grief. My phone line briefly took on the feel of a call centre because of those who constantly checked to see if I was okay.

The Funeral

The atmosphere was one of mixed emotions, but there was no sobbing in the background to starkly contrast the cold atmosphere inside the mortuary. It was Saturday, the 4th of February. And there I was, staring at the body my mom lived in. Her lifeless body still looked as peaceful as she was. I had a flashback to my last meeting with Mom in a cold August. As I knelt on the edge of her bed, mom prayed for my safe return and thanked God for all her children. Even then, the power of our bond could not be broken; saying goodbye seemed like too much to bear.

My eye settled on the face of the embalmed body, lying still in a silver casket. In its lifeless form, Mom's face carried the beauty of serenity.

As I walked alongside my older siblings in and out of the mortuary, reality resurfaced. I have lost my mom! I was beyond tears, and though there was no moisture in my eyes, I still had the dull yet incessant pain in my aching heart.

I was overwhelmed with grave loneliness and tried to remain composed despite the heart-breaking reality that Mom was no longer going to be around.

The Funeral

The morning witnessed troops of family members and friends outside the mortuary to accompany mom's body for a final journey home.

I communicated with family members and relatives, and though gladdened by a reunion after many years, the feeling of loneliness remained. A void settled within me.

As mom's casket emerged from the mortuary, the entire entourage within parked vehicles followed for mom's funeral rites.

Calls and messages hit my phone like the consistent thumping of a butcher's knife on stubborn meat. My phone battery started to run out as old friends wanted to catch up after many years.

Mom's funeral was conducted in three compounds: her paternal, maternal, and husband's residences. My siblings and I were dressed in traditional regalia at our father's residence and were escorted by relatives, along with our nephews and nieces, for a final visit to mom as she lay in state.

As we filed past, I noticed mom's corpse had been redressed with a crown on the head, symbolising a royal paternal descent.

As my eyes left mom's body and rested on one of my nephews, who had lost hold of himself and was gazing at mom's corpse, he was especially grief-stricken by the sight of his beloved grandmother dressed so formally and laid out before us. His facial expression spoke volumes. His thoughts might be different, but his facial expression conveyed the non-verbal communication, "Is this life?" We were engaged in one final moment of reverence and awe in the presence of our departed mom and grandmom.

After paying our last respect, mom's casket was taken to the church, which had been an integral part of my childhood memories. I walked into the same church my mom had dressed me up to attend, but in a different context. I was not there as a little girl dressed up to sing; I returned for mom's funeral service. So many things were familiar, especially the dedicated space where mom sat as she watched me sing.

I was awestruck at the support I got from old friends who left families and businesses to attend mom's funeral. Mom knew most of my old friends and has consistently asked after them during our communications.

My childhood friend, who could not attend, surprised me by sending her niece as a representative with souvenirs. My mother's love and care for her children's friends paid off. My siblings' friends, even friends of my late brother, Prince, left their commitments to attend mom's funeral.

The Funeral

    In times of sorrow and loss, the power of friendship can be truly remarkable. Truly, there is no bond quite like friendship during trying moments in our lives. I am thankful for friends who expended countless hours in prayer with me during the difficulties I faced due to my mother's passing away.

A New Season

Ecclesiastes chapter 3 stresses that life is wrapped up in seasons, and painful seasons undoubtedly beckon hope that spurs the faith to live out the pain. God's grace has accompanied me in my season of transitioning into a full-blown orphan. Perhaps He wanted me to use this time as an opportunity for growth and transformation. I am thankful to God for all things—the good things, the ugly passages, the right paths, and the broken places. There are those who never had the opportunity to have the care of a biological mother. I had one. One who was God's best motherly gift to me. She gave me the nurturing of a good mother. She gave me what no other human could give to me. My mother, though she was my biological mother, also knew me by revelation. I was never a surprise to her, not even on the day I was born. She always had in mind what my purpose and destiny would be. Even when I chose my own path, as most teenagers do, she was not shaken. She knew who I was. As I look back over my life, I see how much God used her to speak into my life—whether I wanted to hear it or not. It is hard for me sometimes not to think that if she

A New Season

were still alive, things would be different. But then, I am quickly reminded of Ecclesiastes 3:1–8 and know that everything happens in its season. There is a time for everything and a season for every activity under heaven. "For everything, there is a season, and a time for every matter under heaven: a time to be born, and a time to die; a time to plant, and a time to pluck up what is planted; a time to kill, and a time to heal; a time to break down, and a time to build up; a time to weep, and a time to laugh; a time to mourn, and a time to dance; a time to cast away stones, and a time to pile stones together; a time to embrace, a time to refrain from embracing; a time to inquire of the Lord."

And so from then on out, every passing day became more meaningful than before; each experience taught new lessons about strength, resilience, and courage, which ultimately allowed me to persevere through grief.

There is indeed a season for everything. And I am learning to embrace the sorrows and joys, the broken places and the mending, the loneliness and the companionship, knowing that God is with me through it all. One day, I will see my mother again. One day, we will dance together in the presence of our Heavenly Father, and everything will make sense. Until then, I press on, embracing this season of orphanhood. Even though at times it didn't feel like it, God never left me during the difficult seasons of my life.

As we navigate through the different seasons of our lives, it is important to remember that God is with us through it all. Even in the midst of pain and sorrow, we can find hope knowing that one day we will be reunited with our loved ones in heaven. Until then, we press on, embracing each season, good and bad, as a part of God's perfect plan for our lives.

Every season comes to an end, and in every end, there is a new beginning. In my season of grief and celebration, I choose to embrace God's grace. Changes may be unfamiliar, but they are certain. Stepping into an unfamiliar season can be challenging because there might be a need to leave behind some ideologies, things, and places that no longer serve a purpose. Understanding the purpose of this transition gave me peace. I know this is not the end.

I am taking one last look back at the edge of my old life before moving forward. Though surrounded by a feeling of familiarity, there was a sense of finality. I thought about how much had changed over the course of this season: relationships lost and many difficult decisions taken. When you are part of God's family, He will go to extraordinary lengths to free you from anything that would stop your ears from hearing His call. In these scenarios, no bonds or obligations can hold Him back, freeing us up for an even more intimate relationship with our Lord and Saviour.

It can be difficult to let go of things, people, and ideologies we are attached to—relationships that no longer serve us well and limiting beliefs. Even though it was challenging at times, there was a sense of calm in knowing these changes were necessary for growth and development.

We must understand that an ending is not always a bad thing. In fact, it is often a good thing because it opens up opportunities for new beginnings. For me, this season of change has been difficult, but I am excited to see what God has in store, and I am grateful for His grace during this transition. God can provide a way to help restore life to anyone facing an unfamiliar change.

The best part is that we can now look forward to the future. Not knowing what lies ahead can be both exciting and daunting, but trusting in God gives me strength during these moments because His plans are always greater than mine. This season has certainly been challenging yet rewarding at the same time. Although there have been plenty of endings along the way, each one opens up more possibilities for better beginnings.

In a better beginning, you find your place in the world when you recognise and nurture the right connections—new connections where solitude is swept away with a newfound sense of unity.

Thanksgiving

As I lay down crying out my heart, my memory caught the soothing voice of my mother asking me to stop crying at my seemingly endless grief after the death of my brother, Prince. I could feel a wave of warmth engulfing me. A year later, Mother, alongside my sister, sat for six hours on the plane to pay me a visit. In the days that followed Prince's departure, grief took over us all. However, God wanted us to find His purpose for each one of our lives through this painful and sorrowful journey in which we found ourselves. He deftly weaves life's circumstances into a tapestry, helping us to cultivate the spiritual abilities necessary for our divine missions. As faith and patience take root within us, God uses them as tools in pursuit of His greater plans. With faith and self-motivation, we can free ourselves from the shackles of sorrow. By submitting to the Lord, an inner transformation awaits us, one that holds the power to renew our strength and give us hope for brighter days ahead.

In the years since my brother's death, and as my grief has slowly transformed into acceptance, I have paused within my emotions to thank God for giving us the mother who fits our life's purpose. With her destiny thrust into ours, we passed through her hands to fulfil our earthly mission.

God, in fulfilling earthly missions, uses earthly vessels. For Jesus, He chose Mary. For John the Baptist, He chose Elizabeth. For Samuel, it was Hannah and for Isaac, Sarah.

As I wiped away the last few tears from my eyes, I thanked God infinitely over and over again because if not, it wouldn't have been possible without Him sending someone special like Mom!

Reflecting on Tributes

Mom's remarkable life has left a lasting legacy marked with conviction, strength of will, and ample courage. While grappling with the pain of saying goodbye far too soon, they found solace in knowing that their experiences with Mom have been truly blessed ones, with so many vivid memories left behind. Fondly called "Sisi," Mom radiated affection towards her nieces and nephews, who attested to the fact that her love for their parents was an inspiration. Mom was an incredibly kind soul who blessed their lives with moments of pure joy and happiness. Many were truly blessed to have encountered Mom and thanked God for the loving relationship they shared with her. Some relatives cited Mom's loving disposition, which will continue to warm their hearts as they cherish memories full of love long after she's gone. Mom had an impactful presence that will be remembered not just by those closest to her but also by all who were blessed enough to experience her generous care and unconditional love towards everyone around her. She truly lived her life as an example of humility before God. Others are comforted by all the shared times and know that eventually they will be united with Mom!

Mom had a soft yet stern way of delivering reprimands to her loved ones who stepped out of line. Known for her exemplary character as the first female matron of Nyemoni Grammar School, Sisi earned great admiration from both students and staff. She was renowned for her peaceful character. Whenever a quarrel arose in the family, she would always intervene with calming words, reminding everyone that only through love can we find true happiness. Her messages conveyed an underlying gracefulness, demonstrating how the strength of character is determined not by force but rather by the pursuit of peace and understanding. Mom's faith remained strong and unwavering in her final hours before she passed into eternal glory. She was described as a "glowing star of beauty and love" with a spirit that touched the souls of all who knew her. For some people, her passing has been a difficult and sudden shock. Her deep devotion to God was clear in the love she showered upon her family, friends, and those around her. Relatives are humbled by her kind-heartedness. Some relatives recounted how Mom strove to give more of herself than anyone else ever did before. They said her gentle words of encouragement and guidance provided strength to the weary and steadied those who stumbled. Nephews remarked that Mom was much more than just an aunt. They are still in shock that this wasn't merely goodbye but also an abrupt conclusion to their shared stage on Earth.

Mom's caring presence proved eternal, even though she has departed. For her grandchildren, she left behind a lasting legacy far beyond the physical. Her legacy of love and devotion will forever be remembered by generations to come. She was a true matriarchal figure who never wavered despite occasional health hiccups. Mom's ever-present smile was a cherished source of love and comfort for her grandchildren. She has left an indelible mark on their hearts for the beautiful moments they shared together. They still long for her infectious smile and warm voice. Sadly, COVID-19 robbed some of them of the chance to see Grandma once more this past year. Although they can no longer bask in magical moments with Mom, they choose to celebrate and cherish all the good memories. They also remember those strict rules of discipline. These treasured recollections will keep serving as a reminder of how truly special Mom was. They described their grandmother as a gift with irreplaceable memories: watching daytime television together, feasting on delicious home-cooked meals while she regaled them with stories from the past. They stated that Mom was an

Reflecting on Tributes

extraordinary woman who enriched their lives with patience, strength, and wisdom while demonstrating unfailing love and generosity towards everyone she held dear. Mom also shared a deep connection with distant relatives.

SIBLINGS' TRIBUTES TO MOM

It is difficult to write about my mother because I am inundated with emotions. I'm inundated with memories of the various qualities that characterize my mother. Sisi, as everyone called her, was a very kind, loyal, dedicated, and loving daughter, wife, mother, grandmother, great grandmother, sister, aunt, cousin, and friend. Rarely do you find people who rejoice with those who rejoice and weep with those who weep, but my mom did so. Not only did she exude joy, peace, and love, but she was also very gentle, kind and patient to a fault. I admired her ability to remain stoic through thick and thin and remain faithful to family and friends who wronged her. She was also very generous with the little she had. I am not a Biblical scholar, but I know that my mother embodied the fruits of the spirit outlined by St. Paul in his letter to the Galatians. She inspired me to realize that lions need not roar for power is made perfect in weakness. I watched my mother of nine bury four of her children, two in infancy and two as adults. I observed the considerable toll on her, but she remained stoic. She raised not only her children but other people's children too. As Matron in three girls' secondary schools, she practically, helped adolescent girls stay focused on their goals and find their ways through the maze of a secondary school education. For many of these girls, it was their first time away from home, so, keeping them focused was quite a daunting task, yet my mother did it with ease. Needless to say, she became second mother to most of them. To my parents, raising children included ensuring that all their children were educated, even with their meagre resources. They also rewarded our curiosity by taking us to places that were not customary, such as visiting Father Christmas at Christmas time. This was a rarity in Nigeria when I was growing up, but they wanted us to have the learning experience. Sisi did not only raise her children but did not hesitate to step in and help her children when they needed her help. She left everything behind when I needed her help and came to the United States, so that I could recuperate and go back to work after the premature delivery of my child. As the child grew and was accepted in day care, she took on part time employment as Customer Service Specialist, first at Caldor's, then, TJ Maxx, and finally, Roche Bros. Sisi remained busy, even as arthritis pain in her knees made it difficult for her to stand for long hours as her job required. She remained faithful, often saying that the Lord's grace was sufficient for her. My mom fasted on

Wednesdays, loved to read the Bible every morning and received communion as often as she could. As I recall her sacrifices as a mother, I remember the following stanzas of a poem I was taught in elementary school

My Mother by Ann Taylor
>   Who sat and watched my infant head,
>   When sleeping in my cradle bed,
>   And tears of sweet affection shed?
>   My Mother.
>   When pain and sickness made me cry,
>   Who gazed upon my heavy eye,
>   And wept for fear that I should die?
>   My Mother.
>   Who taught my infant lips to pray,
>   And love God's holy book and day.
>   And walk in Wisdom's pleasant way?
>   My Mother.
>   And can I ever cease to be
>   Affectionate and kind to thee,
>   Who was so very kind to me?
>   My Mother.
>   When thou art feeble, old, and gray,
>   My healthy arm shall be thy stay,
>   And I will soothe thy pains away,
>   My Mother.

Siblings' tributes to mom

And when I see thee hang thy head,
'Twill be my turn to watch thy bed.
And tears of sweet affection shed,
My Mother.

- Anne Medinus

This special time of celebrating love brings an overflowing emotion as I reflect on all the cherished memories shared with Sisi. From risking life alongside Nigerian Soldiers in order to reunite with family after their civil war, to introducing her to my friends and family during her first visit in Montgomery Alabama - culminating with a joyful trip down Panama City Beach- she never failed at making our birthdays extra memorable by always calling and singing! Let's give thanks for these moments that will forever be held close in heart. Sisi was nothing short of inspirational, with a devotion to the Church that pushed her through thick and thin. Though age had taken its toll on her mobility, she tenaciously made it each week to the doors of Saint Anne in Columbus - every Sunday like clockwork! As if all this weren't enough for one person, Sisi also showed great love and care towards her children; never missing an opportunity for morning chats or goodnight wishes no matter how far away they may have been. Truly a mother's heart knows no limits: thank you so much Sisi!

— *Charles Medinus*

Can this be real? Or is this just a dream? It feels like just a dream; as though you are just asleep. Although I cannot see you, I know you are alive in Christ Jesus... can this be real? We love you mom but God loves you more; hence it turned out this way. A woman of faith, even up until the last minute.

A total mom in all its ramifications. Irreplaceable. Your spirit lives on every single moment and I know that you are walking on the streets of gold right now with the Master; looking down on us all. You are also sitting in Heavenly Places far above everything that has exalted itself above the knowledge of God.Mom, you will always remain our mom- in life or in death.

We can never have a better mom than you. You were the quintessential embodiment of class, industry, wisdom, humour, beauty, peace and transparency.Your spirit lives on mom and we know you are not dead; now amongst the cloud of witnesses. You were a mother of mothers.

You have no equal. God has the answers to all the unanswerable questions regarding your final moments in this world, because we spoke just hours before your departure; and you sounded very strong. Mysteries...but God knows best.

- Patricia Briggs

Sisi you were like a rose that blossomed in the midst of thorns and thistles. Gentle like a Dove yet you soared and weathered every storm like the Eagle. You epitomised faithfulness and fidelity in marriage. As a virtuous woman your price is far above rubies. Godliness, neatness, contentment and mannerism were some of the virtues we learnt from you. Step children, those of your relatives and all others around you were fostered like your biological children. From being a School Matron in Nigeria to working as the best sales Representative in the United States , you displayed diligence worthy of emulation. Ascribing all glory to God, I say a big Thank You for the uncommon motherly blessings you poured on me, my wife, Mildred and our children before leaving for the United States. Expressing great joy over every little success we made was indeed a source of encouragement. I also learnt from you that meekness is not weakness. Truly the Lord disappointed the expectations of those who conspired to pierce your family with many sorrows as you lived a fulfilled life and your departure is but a celebration of life. Besides, weeping may endure through the night but joy comes in the morning. With Our Lord Jesus as the captain of your salvation, I'm sure that it is the morning of your life in heaven. On the morning of October 3rd, 2022 when the news of your passing on to glory was confirmed to me, I said to the Lord " what ever my loss, thou has thought me to say it is well with my soul ". "The Sisi !" as I fondly hailed you, I will miss you, my loving mother. Rest in the bosom of the Lord until we meet at the feet of Jesus. Amen. Sisi dein na mu. Your loving son.

Godson Medinus

A Final Word

We all leave our mark on the world in some way or another—what legacy will you create? What kind of lasting impression are you crafting with your choices today and every day that follows?

Women have the power to do amazing things for God's kingdom. Don't let anyone tell you otherwise! Let your voice be emboldened and show that, despite any obstacles in our paths, we are capable of making a lasting difference.

Ready to break out of your rut? Don't let life simply pass by. It is time for action. Make every moment meaningful! Reach beyond yourself and your fears to create a life full of purpose, helping those around you as much as possible.

ABOUT THE AUTHOR

Peculiar Medinus is the youngest daughter of Mrs. Molly M. Benibo, who sadly passed away a night after speaking with her. Though devastated by her mom's death, Peculiar was inspired to write a short memoir in her mom's memory.

Peculiar's other books include *Single Act, Female Preacher, Never Get Hurt, Lady Battle Axe, Overcomer, The Quickest Way to Overcome Stress, Pray without Straying, Expose, Synopsis of Health and Beauty,* and *The Bunch.*

Peculiar's books are intended for readers looking for motivation on how best to navigate life's many challenges.

www.ingramcontent.com/pod-product-compliance
Lightning Source LLC
Chambersburg PA
CBHW020427010526
44118CB00010B/451